Guided By Grace

Letters to the Lord

Marie Elizabeth Manning

BookLeaf
Publishing

India | USA | UK

Made with ❤ on the BookLeaf Publishing Platform

www.bookleafpub.in

www.bookleafpub.com

Dedication

Dedicated to Grace Community Church
Thank for always seeing me and loving me
To my Mother
Thank you for getting me to church
Love you

Preface

This book is a collection of poems about My Faith
The experience I have gained
The challenges I have faced
The feelings I have endured
And the love I have accepted
Good or bad
This life is mine

Acknowledgements

Special Thank You
D'Shan Berry
Vladimir Anorve
Helen Walters

1.

1. Hard Knock Life

Dear God,

It's been a day, a week, a year. How precious every moment I live for you can be. Did you see me today, trying my best? Giving my all to the world. Sometimes, I don't feel good enough to have the blessing you lay out for me. I get angry about the things I can't control but remember to let you handle the trials. Do you ever get angry? Did you ever feel alone?

I take time to sit with you always. In hopes it will help me grow.

P.S. Heavenly Hugs
Marie

2. Hang ups

Dear God,

I can't stop thinking about the people I love, that are now with you. Do you hold them as dear as I do? Does my mom make you laugh? Does Ross talk your ear off about great music and movies? Is my Uncle Jono making you drink tequila or go out for a motorcycle ride? Did my Aunt Glenda make you red beans and rice? I do cry and wonder why you needed to call them home. Maybe it's because you were feeling all alone. The Angels that are with you now, are apart of who I am. I am so glad that you made me and made sure I had them.

P.S. I Miss You
Marie

3. Habits

Dear God,
I don't want to drink too much. I don't want the imprint
of my families habits to go inside of me. I worry all the
time that the cycle will come back around. I know you
keep me busy, and true joy I have found in that. But am I
staying busy or running from my worries? Will I slip and
fall into the darkness, that has eaten at my family.
Memories of having fun, laughter, holidays and birthdays
too. But the memories soaked in alcohol like it was the
normal thing to do.

P.S. Ease My Worries
Marie

4. Hurts

Dear God,
Why is it so hard for me to make friends? Ones that
don't abandon me or make me feel ashamed. I go above
and beyond for people that I never should. Are you
teaching me something about not giving so much of
myself? I wish I did not care, like so many that I know.
But feeling love and accepted for all my quirks, shouldn't
hurt this much. Friendships are something I've struggled
with since I was a child. Just wanting to fit in. And to
feel as cool as all the other kids.

P.S. Friends Forever
Marie

5. Consume

Dear God,
Why do I have an endless hunger that lives inside of me?
The comfort of each bite, makes me feel at peace. I know
that we should feed our soul spiritually and stay true.
But this hunger that grows inside of me, is something I
want to break through. My body is a Temple, so why
can't I just stop. Drowning in my sorrows with every
sweet, and savory dish that comes up. Each day I reflect
on loving myself more. The binge bond will be broken.
Another day to be grateful for.

P.S. Fill my soul
Marie

6. Mamas Baby

Dear God,
I may not be a mom on earth, but heaven knows my struggles. I thought I wasn't good enough to be a Mama Bear. So, I never questioned why things happen. My mom has babies in heaven. So many women do. I cried and cried but never questioned why. Was there something wrong with me or maybe not the right time? I cherished the possibilities but never faced the grief. So hold my baby tight, and one day I will see. Mamas little baby as happy as can be.

P.S. Sealed with a kiss
Marie

7. La Musica

Dear God,

Thank you for putting music in my life. Hearing my mom sing at The Hop is something I remember well. The Star Dog and Blues Bar cafe open mics is where we all would share. Learning to create helped with the pain.

The pain so many of us hold among the torment of adolescents, like no one understands. The rhythm, the beats, the melody are still ringing strong inside my head. An outlet I hold so close. Sharing my stories through my music is healing to me.

P.S. John Prine
Marie

8. Community

Dear God,
I feel so overwhelmed with joy. To know I have neighbors I can count on. I know I will never go hungry or be alone if I need someone. It's hard to connect to others but if you try you will be surprised. You can find kind people around, if you need a helping hand. Being vulnerable can be scary but community is important to me. To feel connected to something in this big wide world, makes things feel at ease.

P.S. Cups of sugar
Marie

9. Holidays

Dear God,
The holidays were filled to the brim. With laughter,
liquor and lots of food. My grandma had ten kids, so
holidays were like a circus. Chocolate covered cherries
and black olives on my finger tips. Grand kids would line
up in a row to get a lucky Two Dollar bill. But grandmas
now in heaven, my aunts and uncles too. So, holidays are
hard, but my memories get me through.

P.S. Leftovers are the best
Marie

10. Over The Edge

Dear God,
I have felt desperate enough to be with you. To cut what
life I have short and not let my destiny follow through. I
stop to remember how blessed I really am. I try to run
from the darkness, that calls to me. But something gets
me sucked back in. Loneliness and anger, the victim that
weighs me down. I pray to you in these times of
desperation. You remind me I am built to be courageous,
calm, caring and loved.

P.S. Strength
Marie

11. All The Colors

Dear God,

My mom taught art when I was growing up. Thank you for blessing her with that gift. I remember all the colors in the tie dye tapestry she'd make, like a super nova in the sky. She would make hubcaps into clocks. And was even featured on CBS Sunday morning for her recycled art. I used to be embarrassed of having a mom so open and different. Now I reflect on the art she shared and her students that stuck with it. Thank you for creating a world where people can express themselves. Through all the colors of the rainbow. Each as special as the next.

P.S. The Yucca Center
Marie

12. Sundays

Sundays are for families and giving praise to God.
Sunday morning sermons take communion flesh and
blood. Glory to the kingdom of heaven, hold my hands
up high. Wash away my sins and wipe my crying eyes.
Lost and broken without you. Inviting you into my heart.
Comfort light surrounding as I step out of the dark.

P.S. I worship you
Marie

13. Texas

Dear God,
How do you pick what family we will have? Or the places we are born? Or the love that we receive? The state I am from is a place I hold fond memories. Crawdad fishing on warm summer nights. Swimming at the Lake Worth and sandy sandwiches made on the cooler. Grass stains on my knees from football in the park. And Sunday School at First Baptist made me a Awana Sparks Kid.

P.S. Texas Tornado
Marie

14. Past Prisoner

Dear God,

My past was like a ball and chain. I would drag it along with me, like it had to remain. We all have pasts that can make us feel broken. I've been a prisoner of my past for too long. Stepping away from the burden is like walking in quick sand. The faster I walk the more I sink. The slower I stroll the more to learn and heal from. Can you send me patience and peace? I want to be free.

P.S. Brave Heart
Marie

15. Little Big Kid

Dear God,

Why do we all want to grow up so fast? No time to enjoy being young. Chasing responsibility and trying to make a way. Each generation so different, yet completely the same. We want guidance, love, understanding and stability. Half of us so tired, we have given up. The others pouring into empty cups. I want to feel completely full and content. Why did I think growing up would solve so many youthful problems? The only true problem is letting your inner child go.

P.S. Take me back
Marie

16. John 1:1

Dear God,
The church bus would always pull into the apartments
where I grew up. Sunday mornings, Wednesday nights
grab my Bible and hop in. The joy I felt when I joined the
Lord's Army made me feel like I finally found my home.
No one could take you away from me. You never left my
side. I asked you to forgive me of my sins and live inside
my heart. How wonderful to know you. How wonderful
to honor you, praise you and love you.

P.S. In the beginning
Marie

17. Ministries

Dear God,
You give us all so many gifts to share with the world. So much uptapped potential and possibilities. The insecurities can hold us back. The fear of failure can get in our way. We need to look at the signs. Let our faith ease the unsteady waves we create within ourselves. Give us all the strength to see the power we hold. Help change our minds, so we can change the world.

P.S. Impactful
Marie

18. Take The Wheel

Dear God,
How delusional can we all be to think we are in control?
Take me by the hand and tell me it will be ok. I want no
worries, no grey hairs or wrinkles around my eyes. But I
grind my teeth at night, making lists for the next day.
Thinking if I have a little plan no stress will come my
way. But sometimes nothing goes to plan and the world
still keeps spinning. But why do I feel like my face is on
fire, when things don't go the way I played it out in my
head?

P.S. Major Tom to ground control
Marie

19. Here I Am

Dear God,

It's such a relief to have nothing to hide. You know who I am and all the pain I carry. I don't need to feel bad about being sad. I wish I felt comfortable enough to be vulnerable with someone again. To share how I feel with some family or friends. I noticed as I try to share, people just stay away. No one wants to be burdened with my loss and loneliness. Yet, I embrace the glory of knowing you. You made me relentless in the pursuit to be content.

P.S. All together lovely

Marie

20. Glorieta

Dear God,
Growing up, I attended Fellowship of Christian Athletes.
Those were some of the best times of my childhood.
Worship, retreats and walking toward the next chapters
in my faith. So much hope for a teen with the weight of
the world. Peer pressure, broken home. A place in chaos
I find peace. Blessed for the teachers who love God and
facilitate this beautiful thing.

P.S. Every move I make
Marie

21. Rebirth

Dear God,

Thank you for giving me life twice: the day that I was born and the day I chose to be born again. Chosen from a starry milky way. A shining light that grows with each day I continue to glorify you. I lift you up. I sing your name. I will never squander the purpose you have placed in my path. The end is never near, when granting me eternal life.

P.S. My soul to keep

Marie

www.ingramcontent.com/pod-product-compliance
Lightning Source LLC
Chambersburg PA
CBHW051002030426
42339CB00007B/441